Moms and Babies

Written by Vicky Shiotsu
Illustrated by Roberta Collier Morales

On a hot, hot plain
in the swishy, swishy grass,

lion and her babies cuddle.

In the cold, cold Arctic
in an icy, icy cave,

polar bear and her babies huddle.

On a high, high mountain
up a snowy, snowy cliff,

bighorn and her baby leap.

In the dry, dry desert
on the gritty, gritty sand,

camel and her baby sleep.

In the deep, deep ocean
through the quiet, quiet waters,

whale and her baby glide.

In a wet, wet marsh
near some tall, tall reeds,

duck and her babies hide.

In a cool, cool forest
from a sturdy, sturdy branch,

opossum and her babies swing.

In a thick, thick jungle
up a leafy, leafy tree,
monkey and her baby cling.